HALLOWEEN CAT
COLORING BOOK FOR TODDLERS

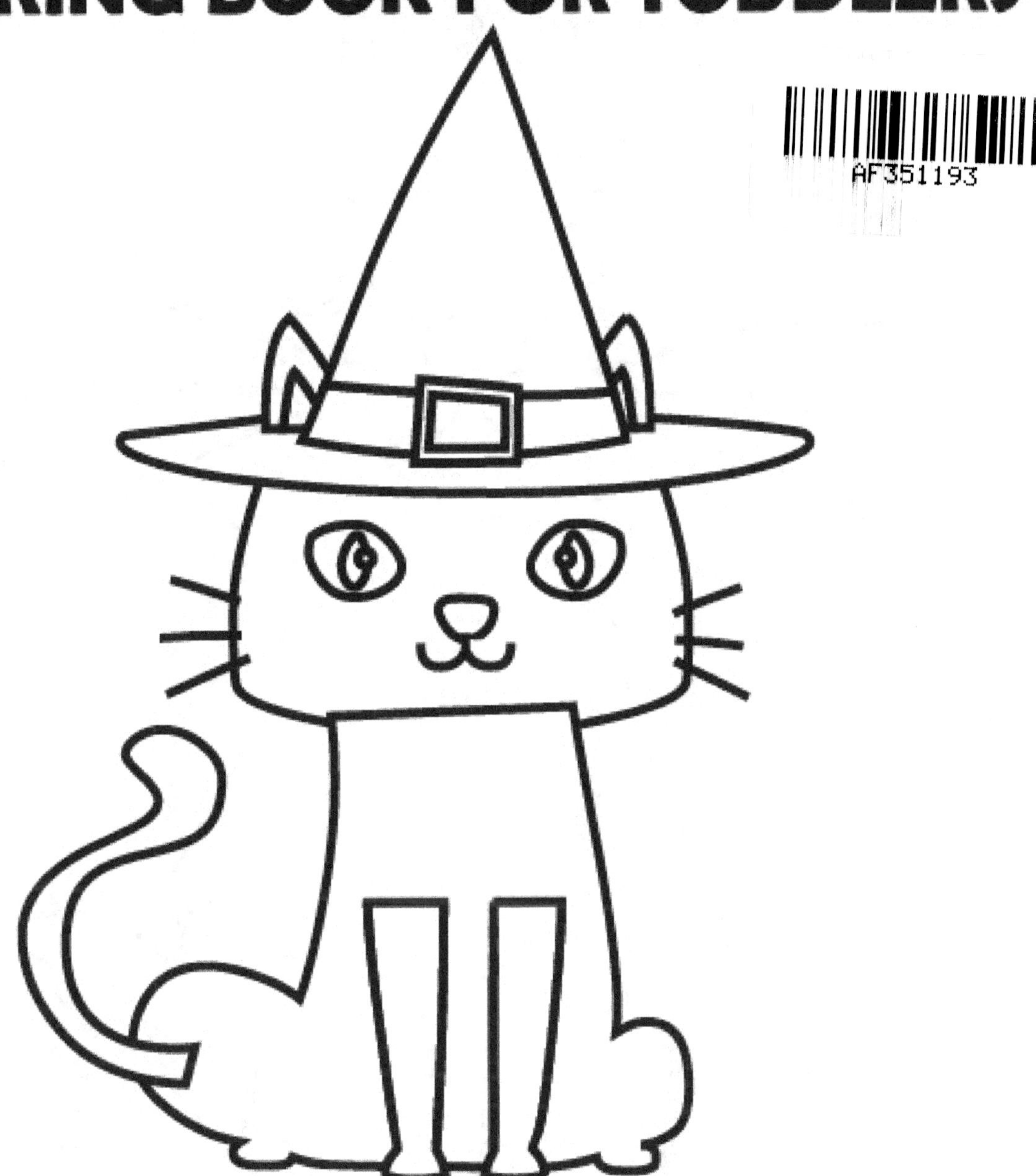

THIS BOOK BELONGS TO:

____

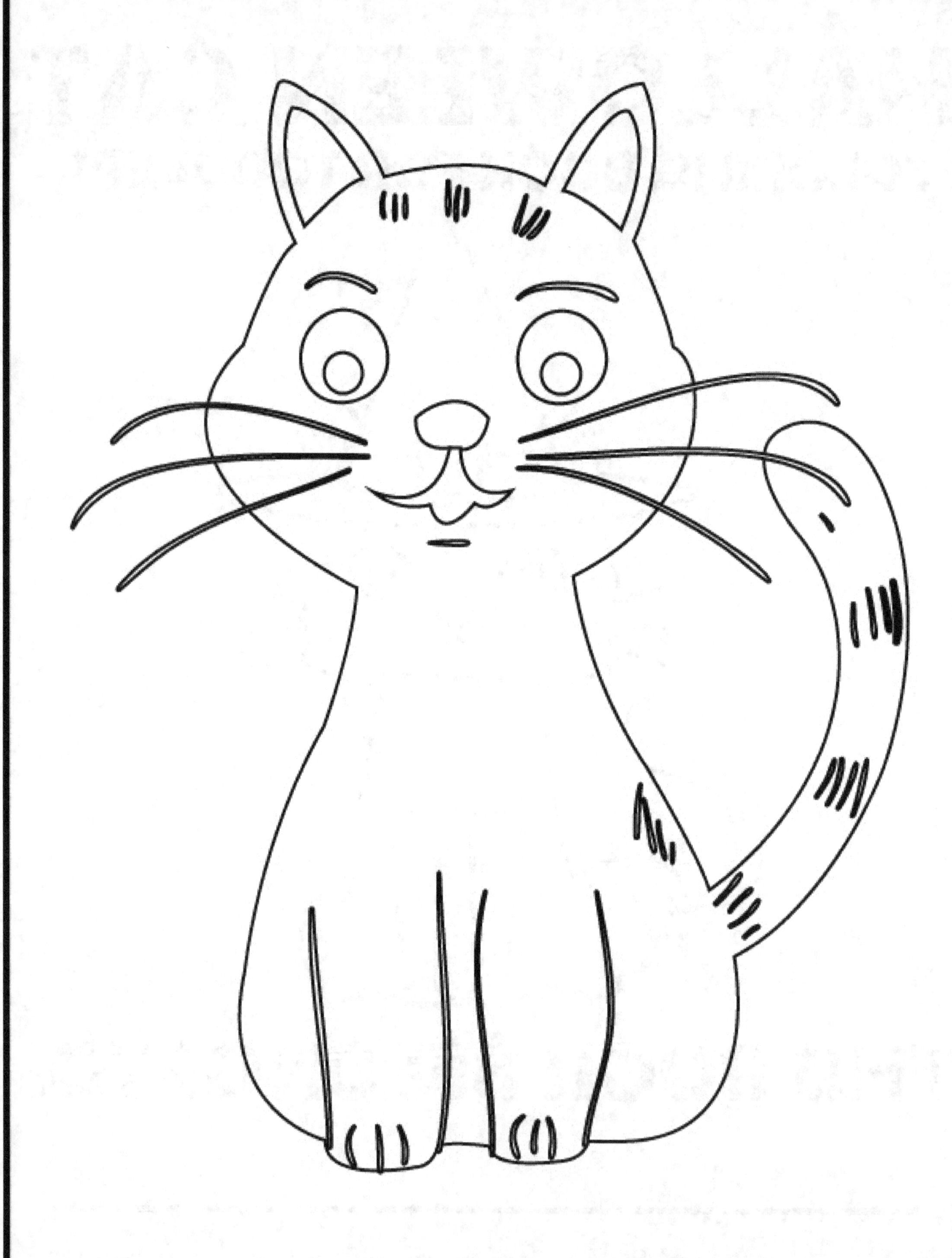

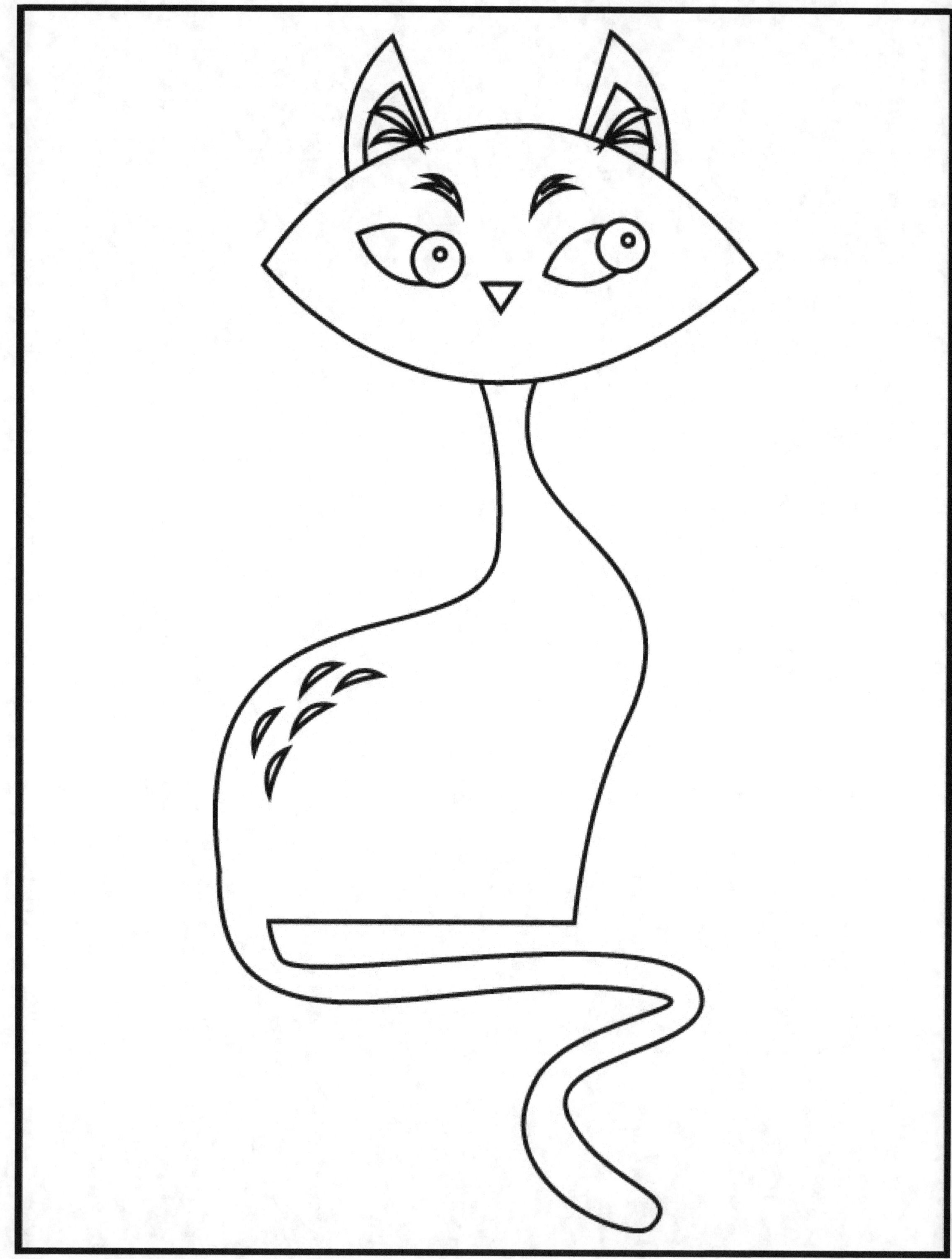

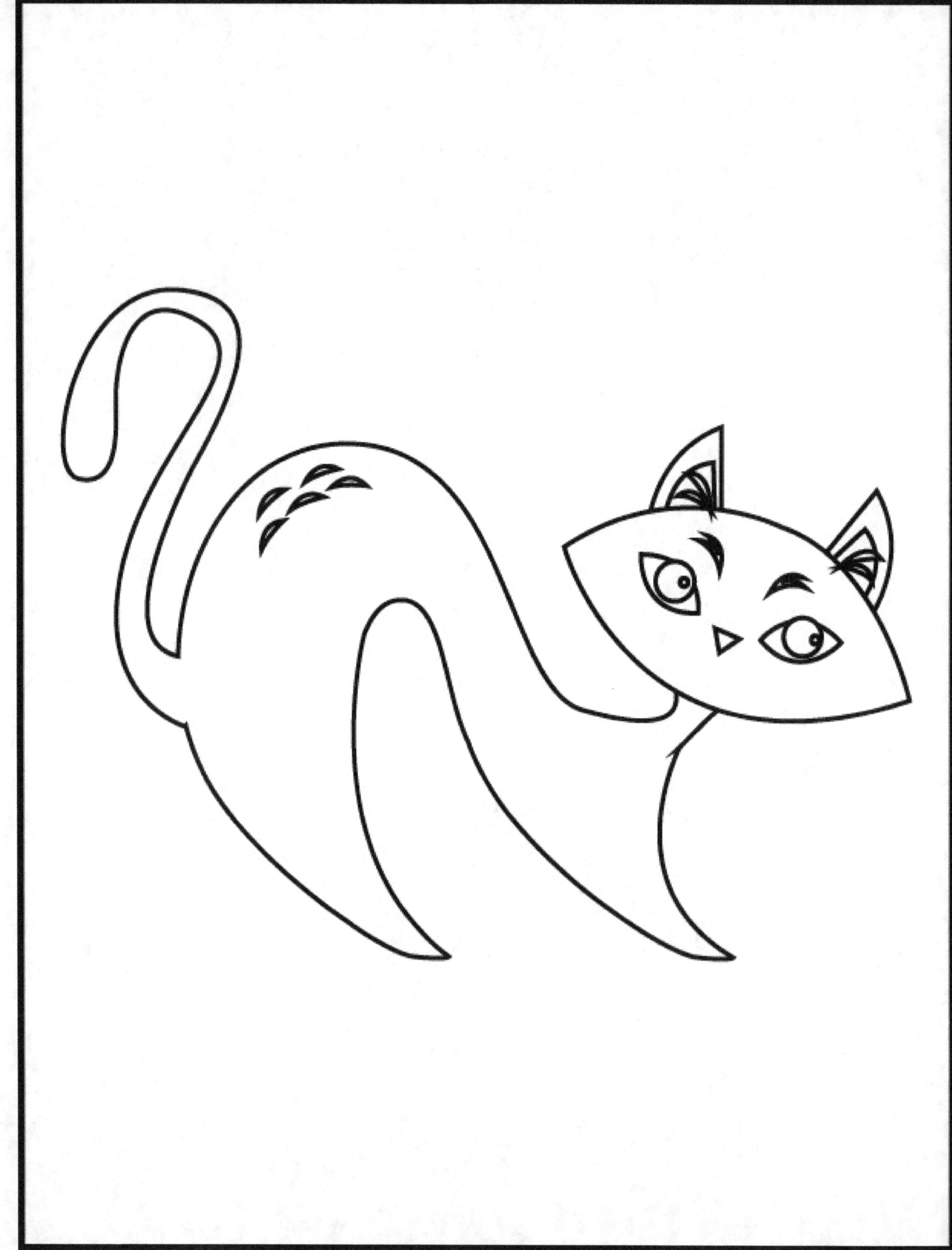

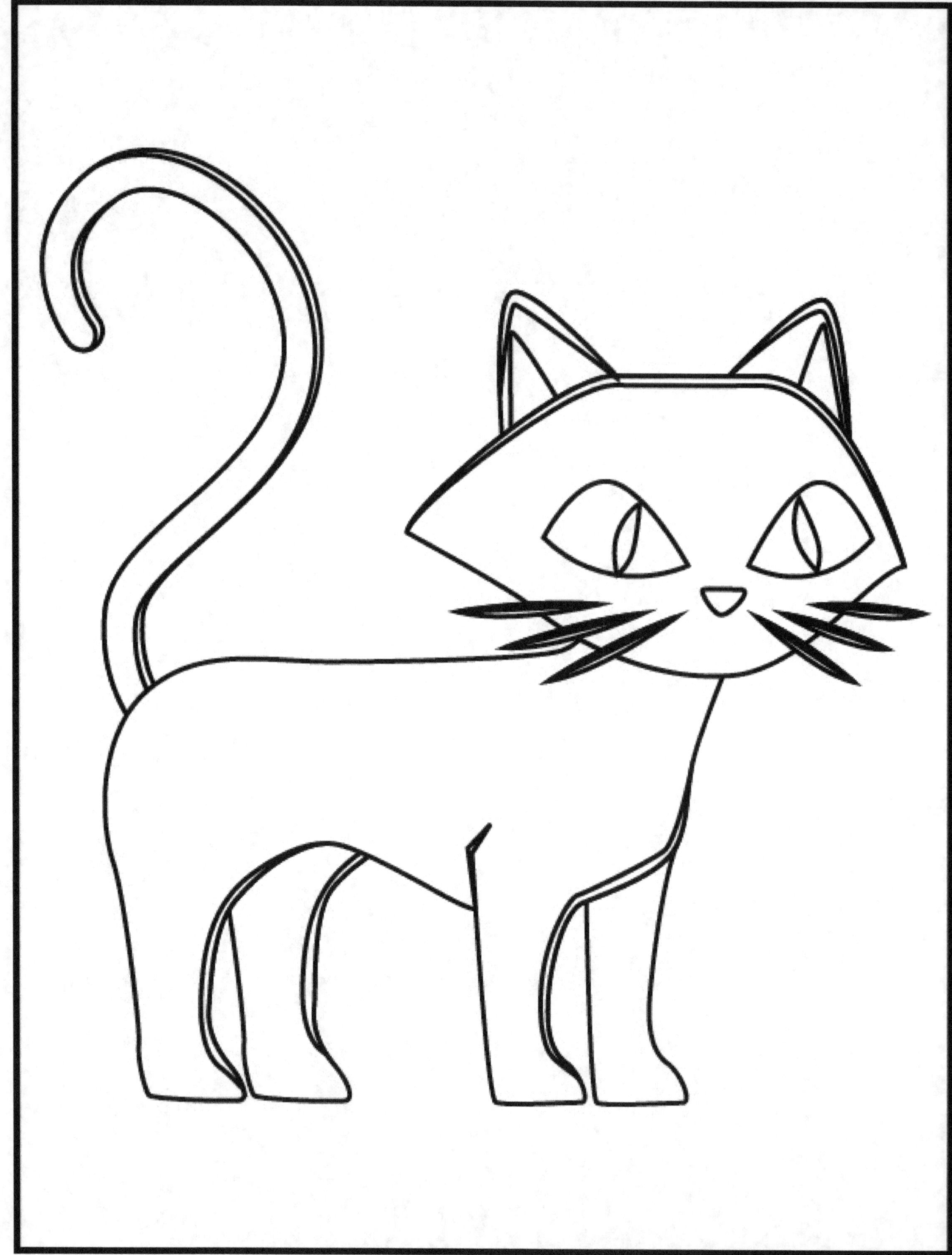

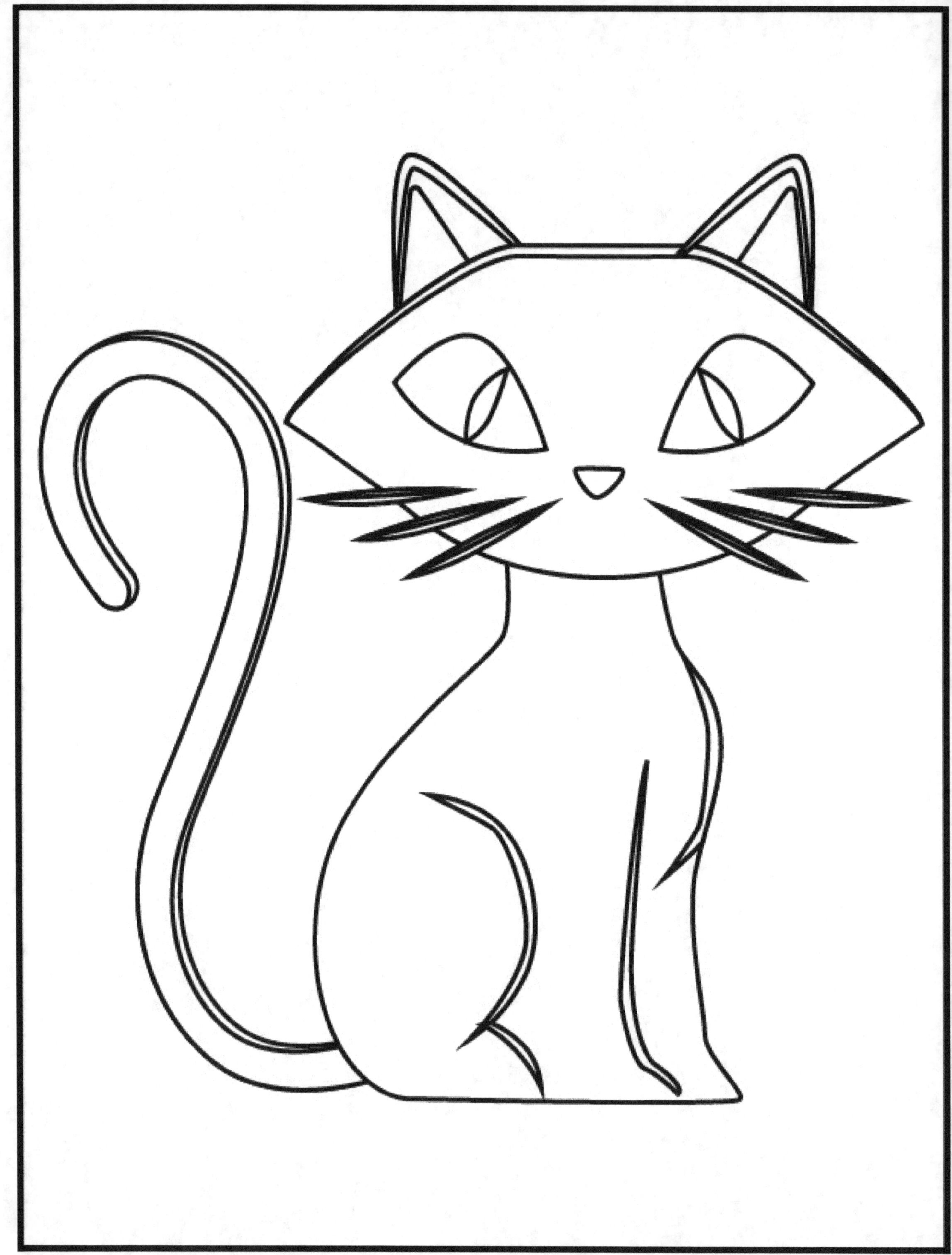

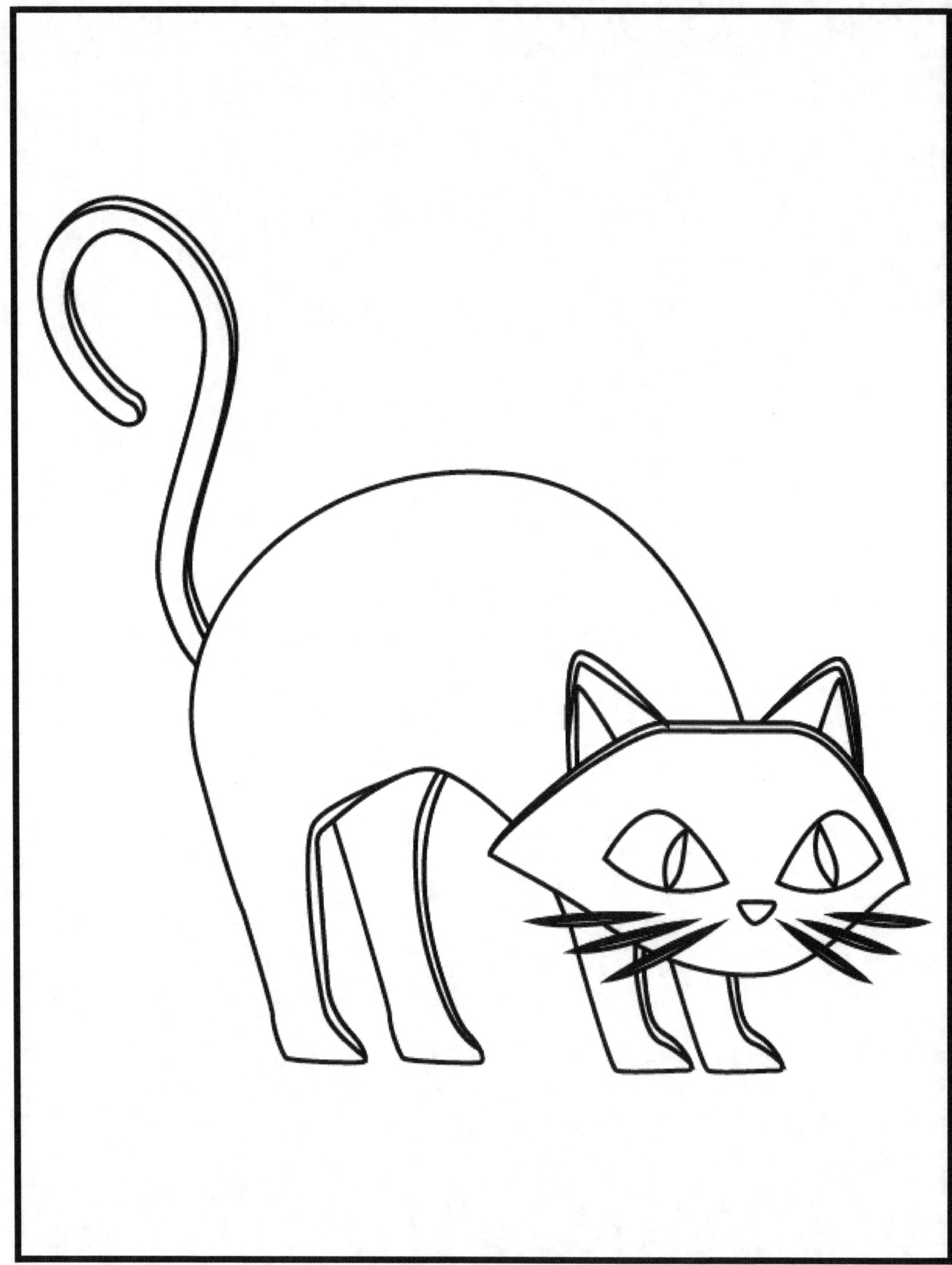

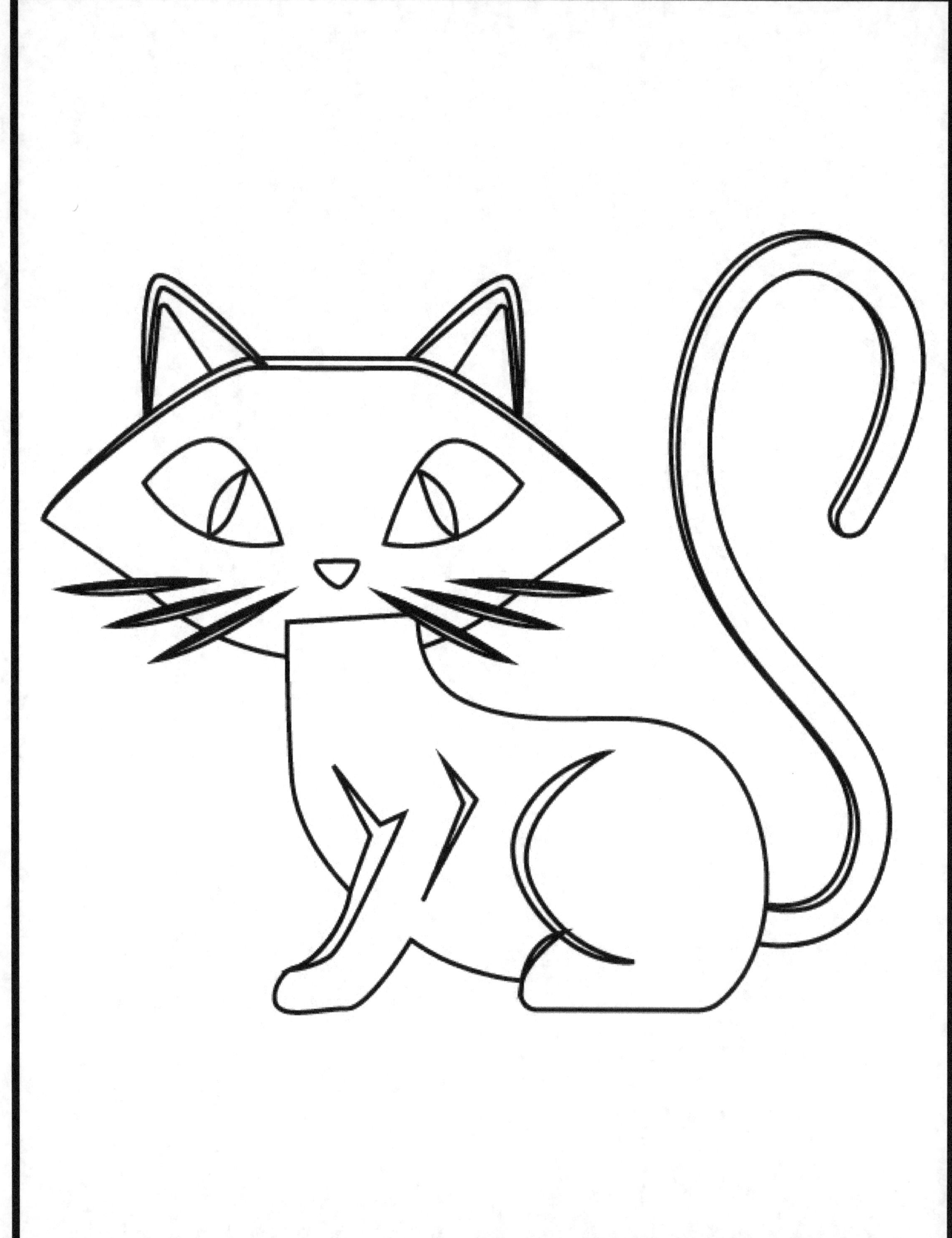

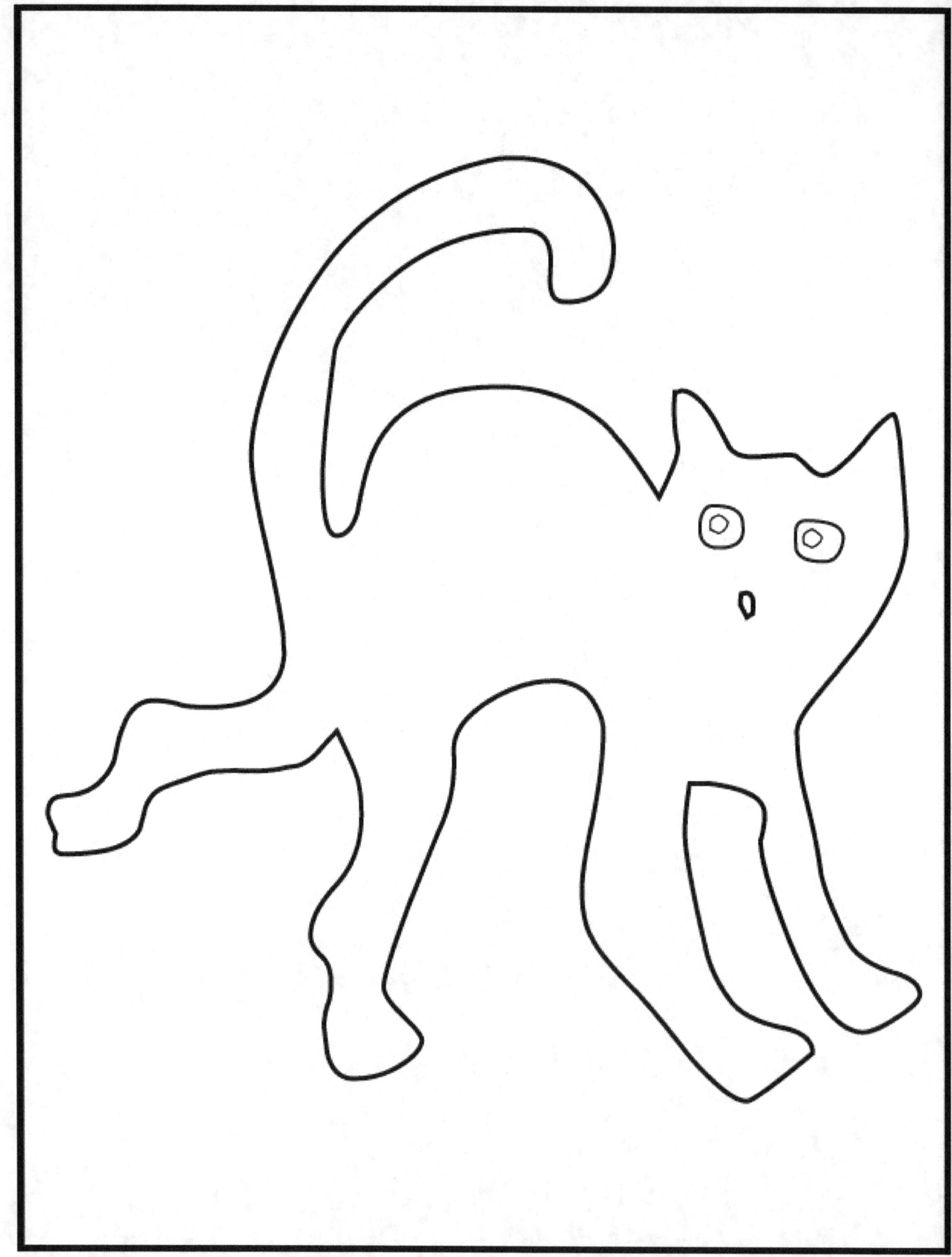

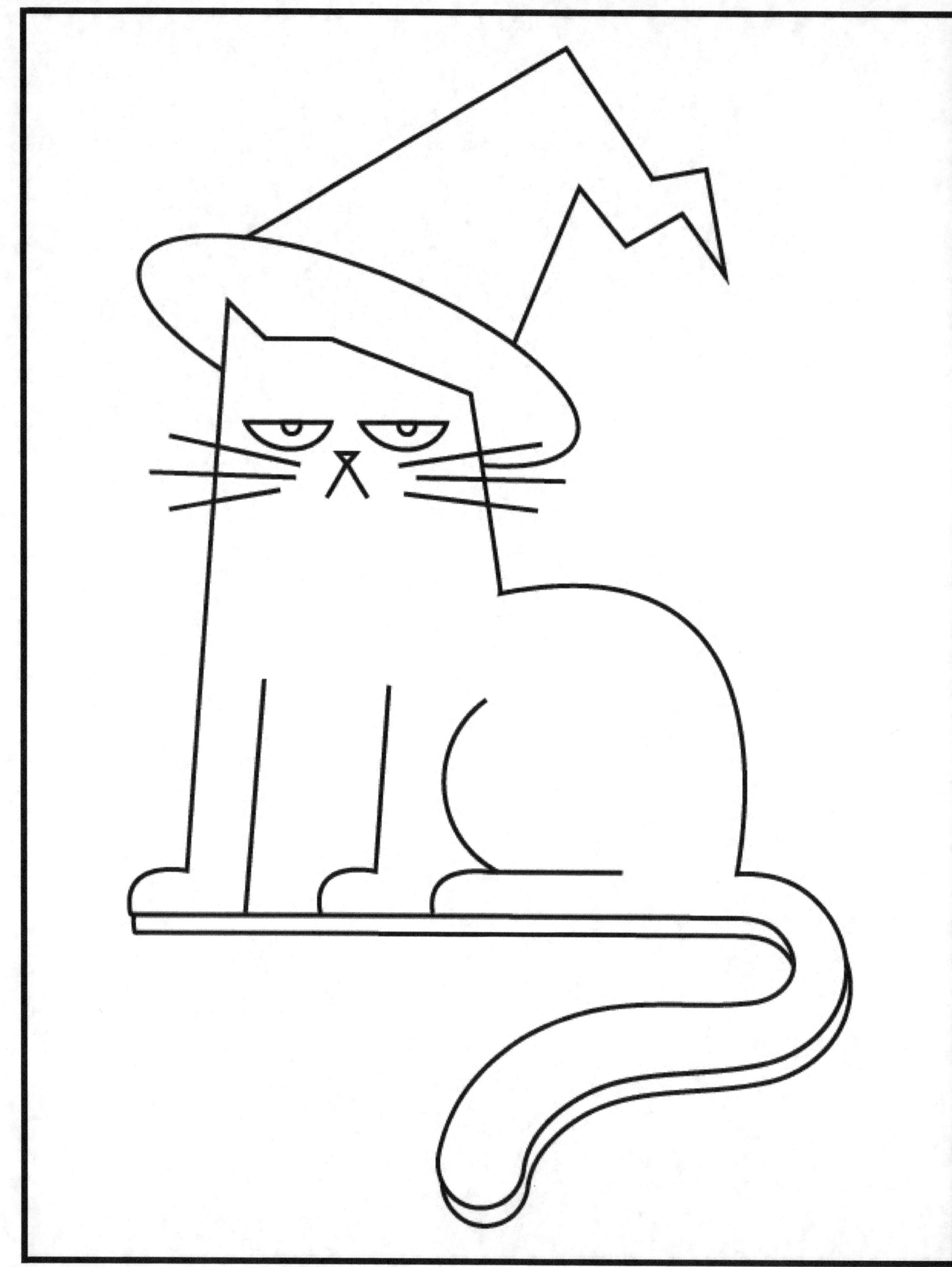

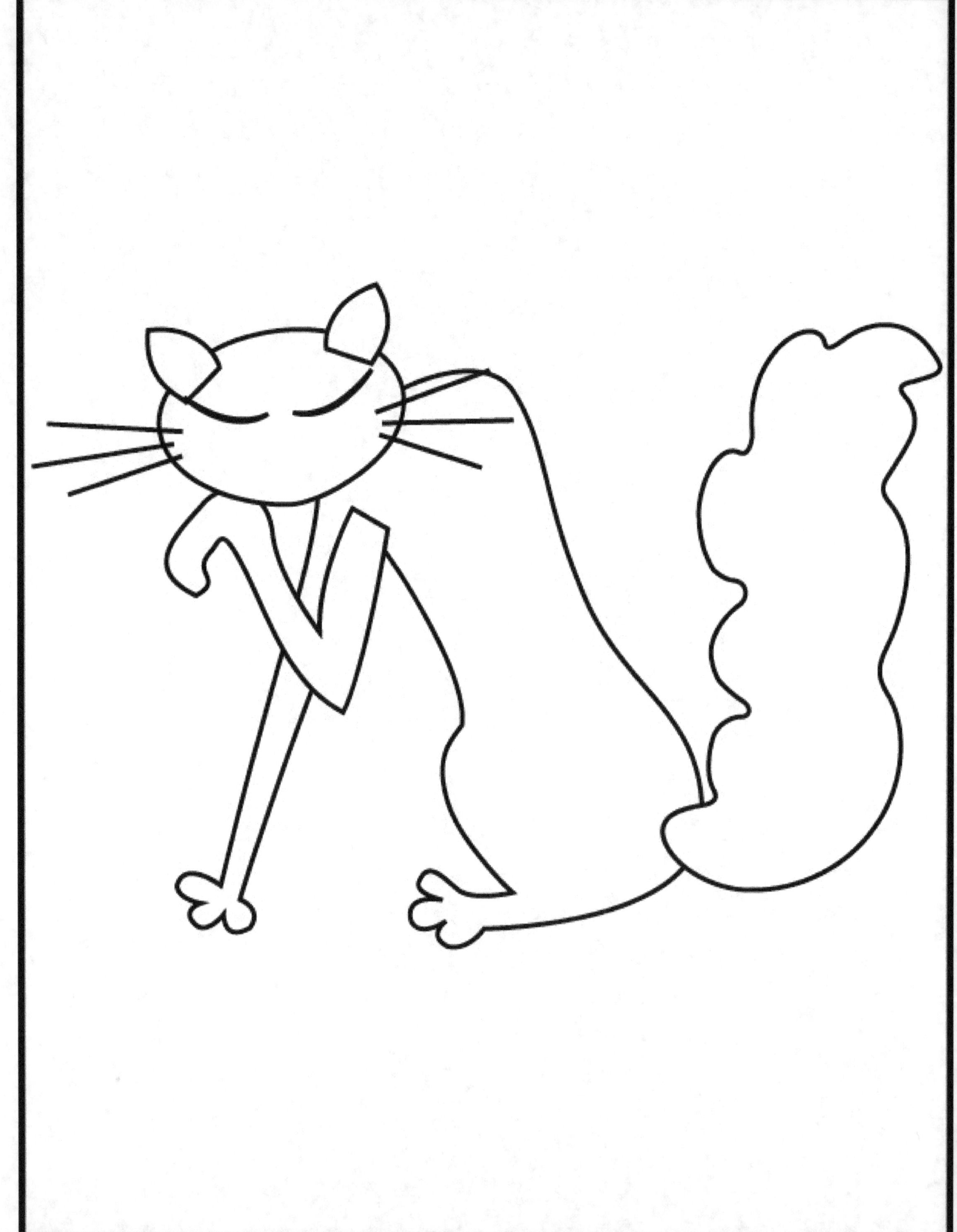

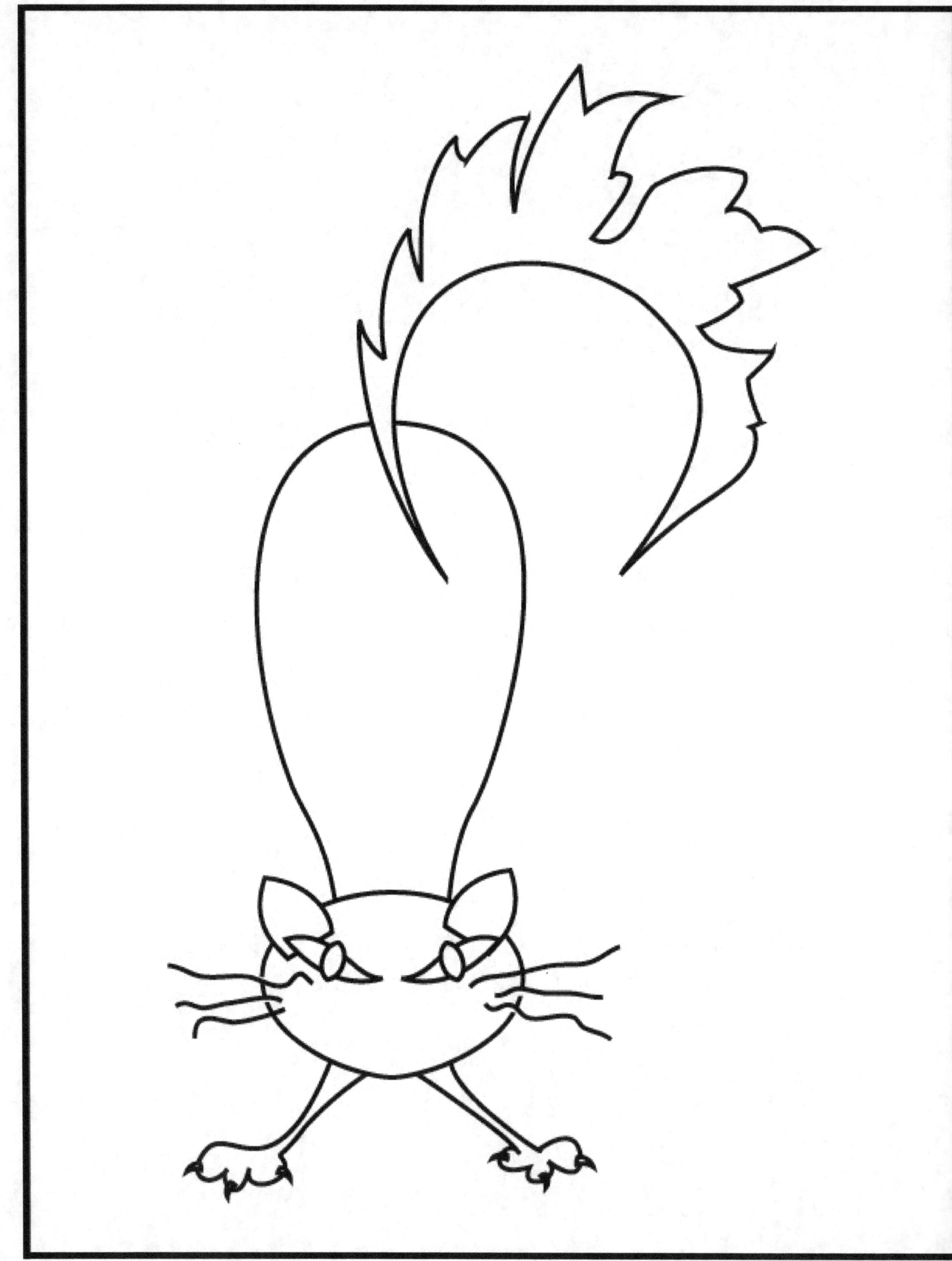

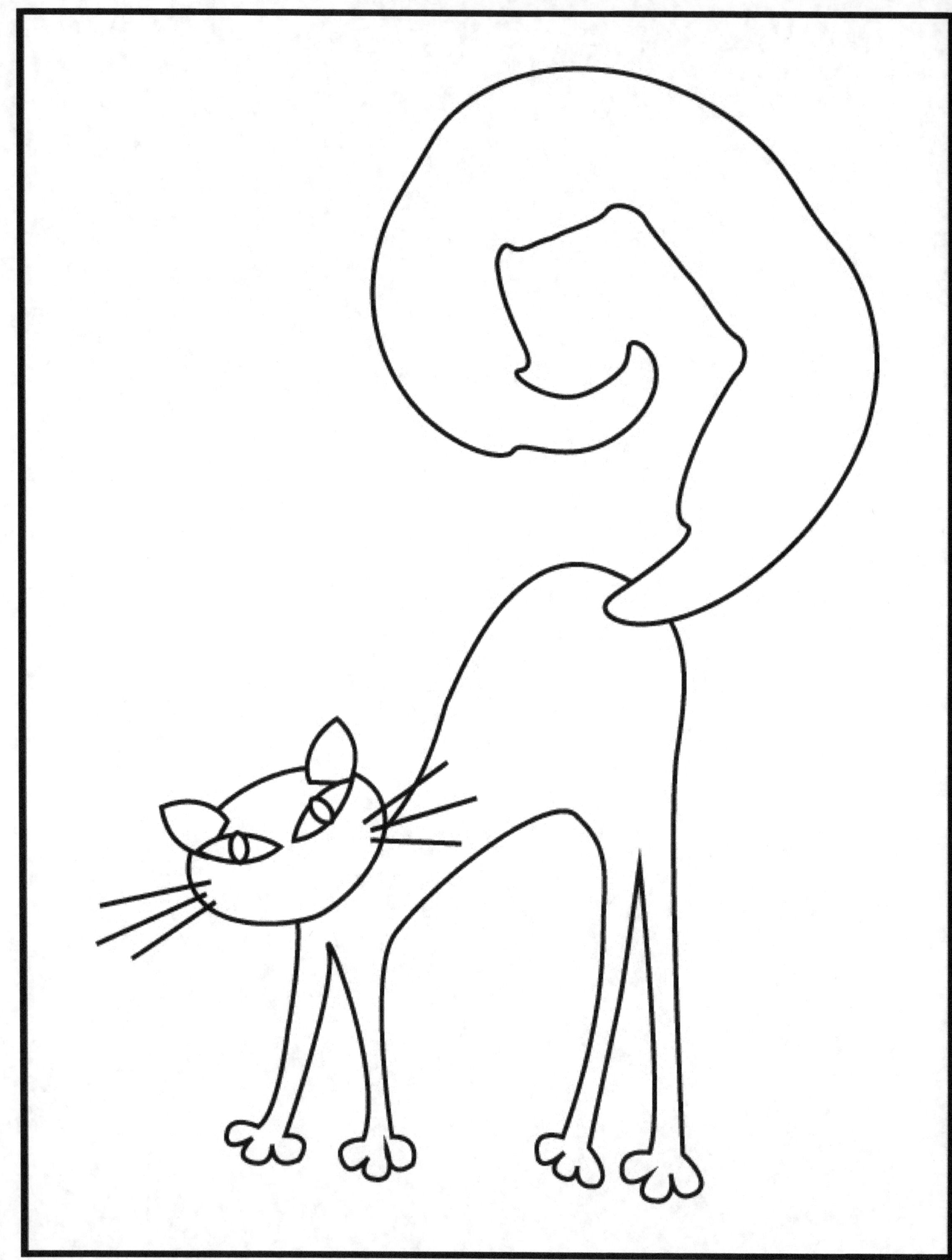

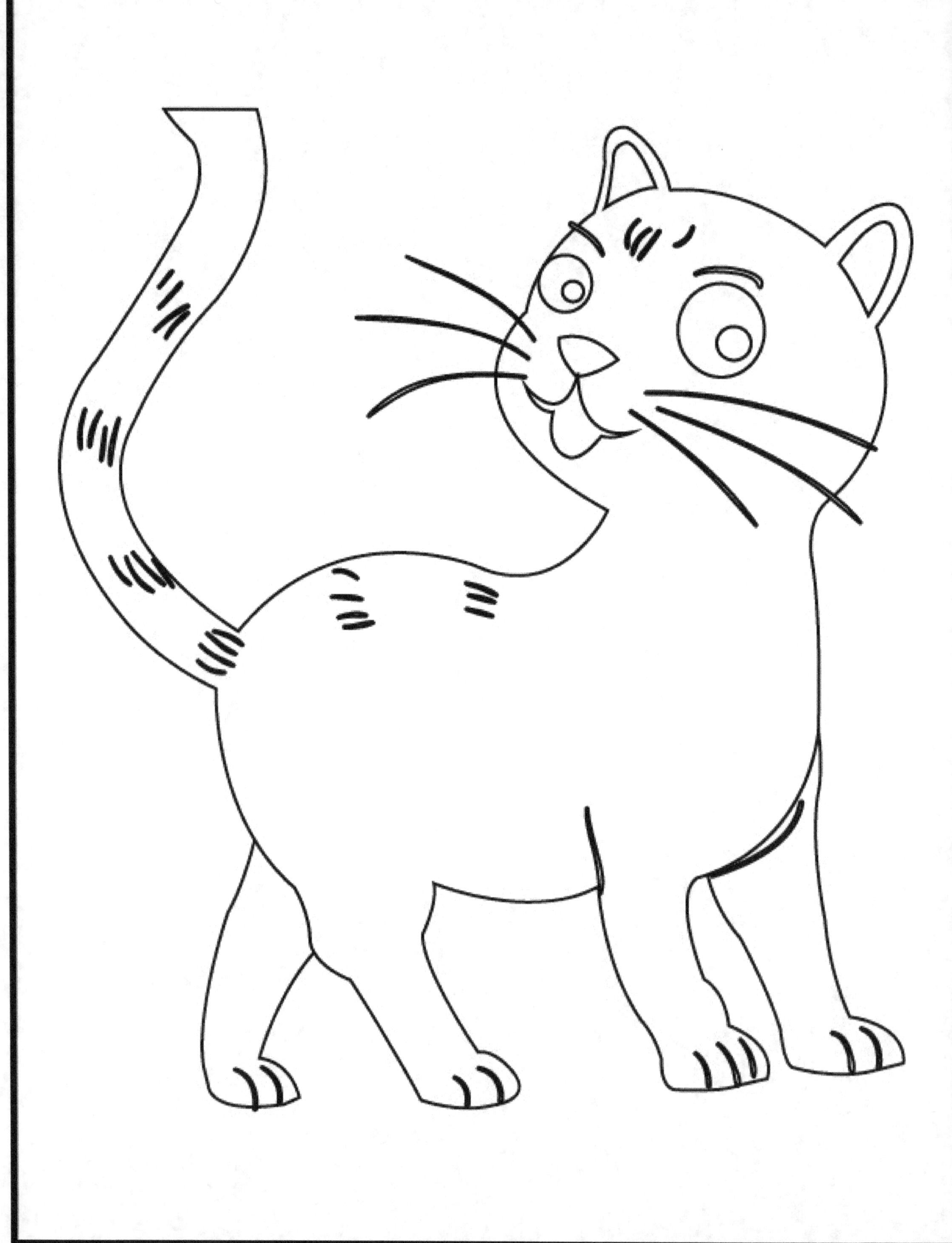

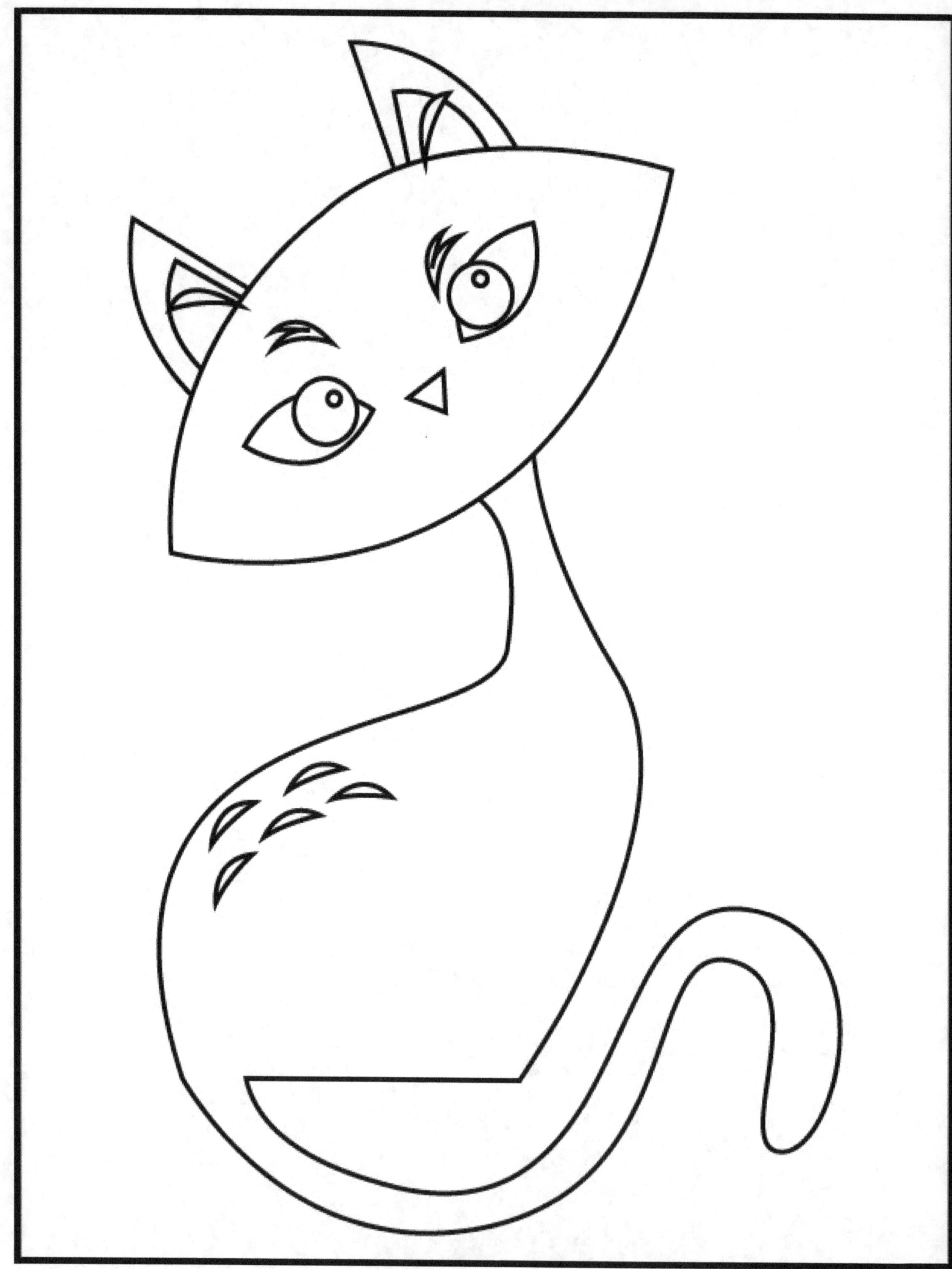

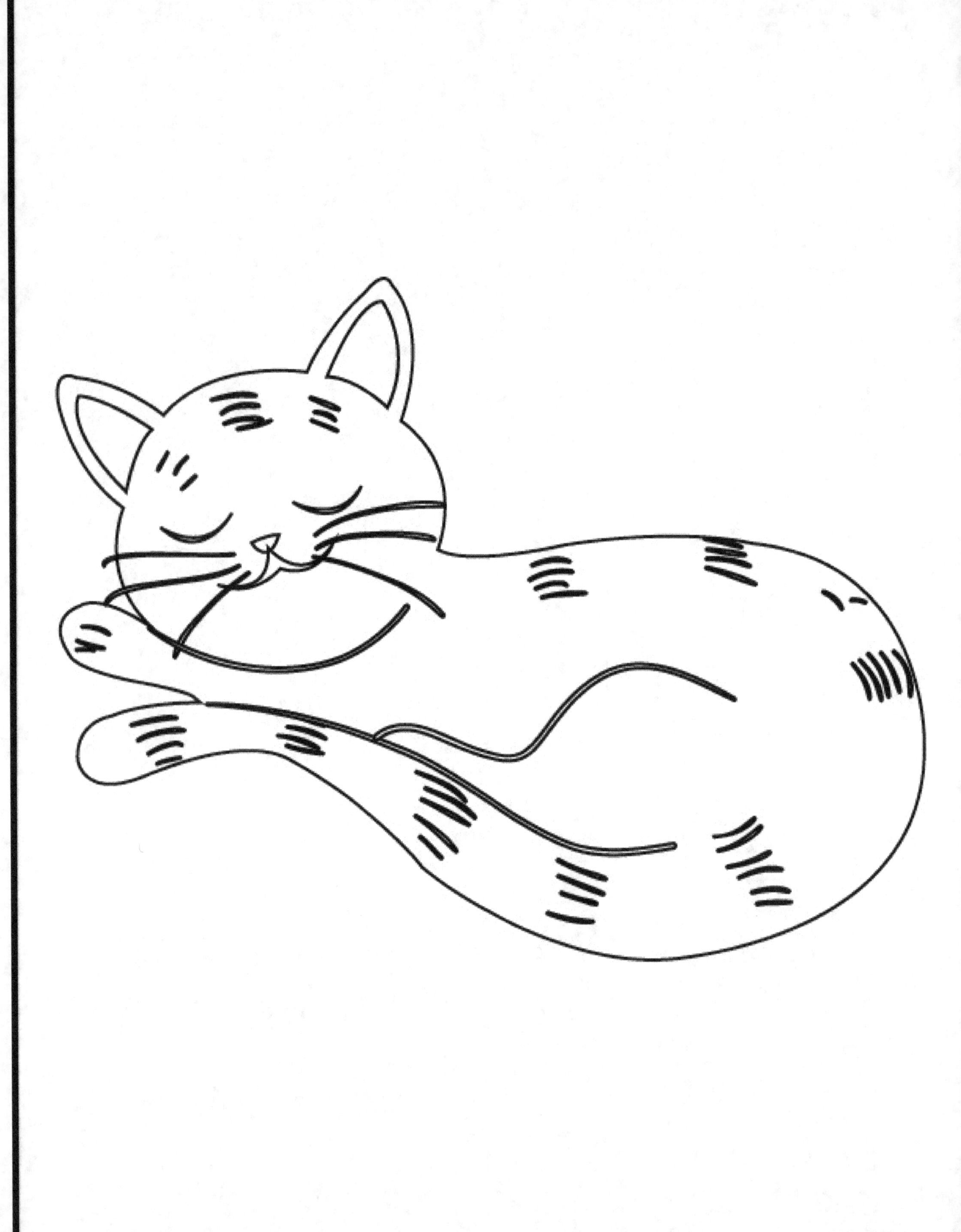

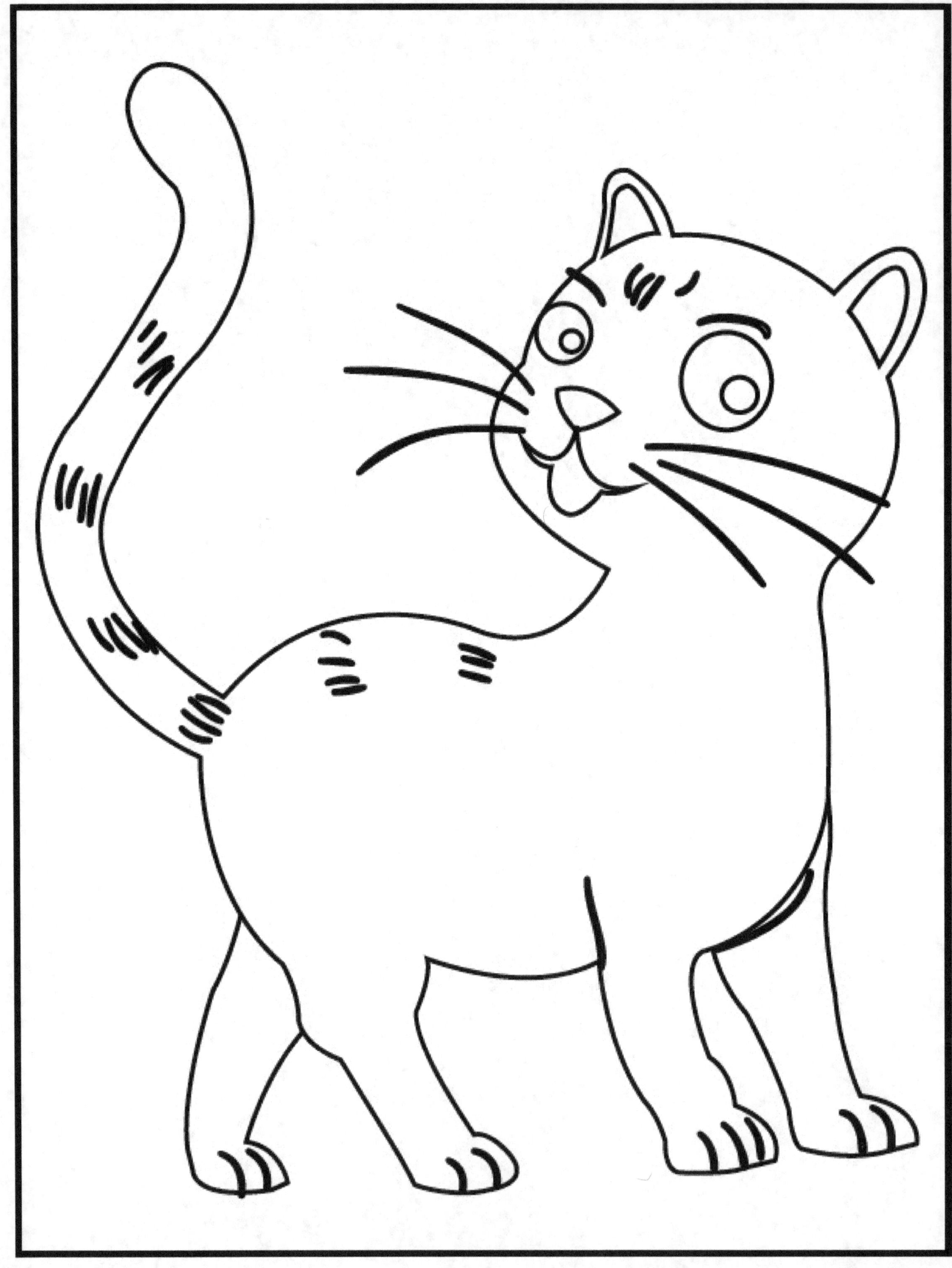

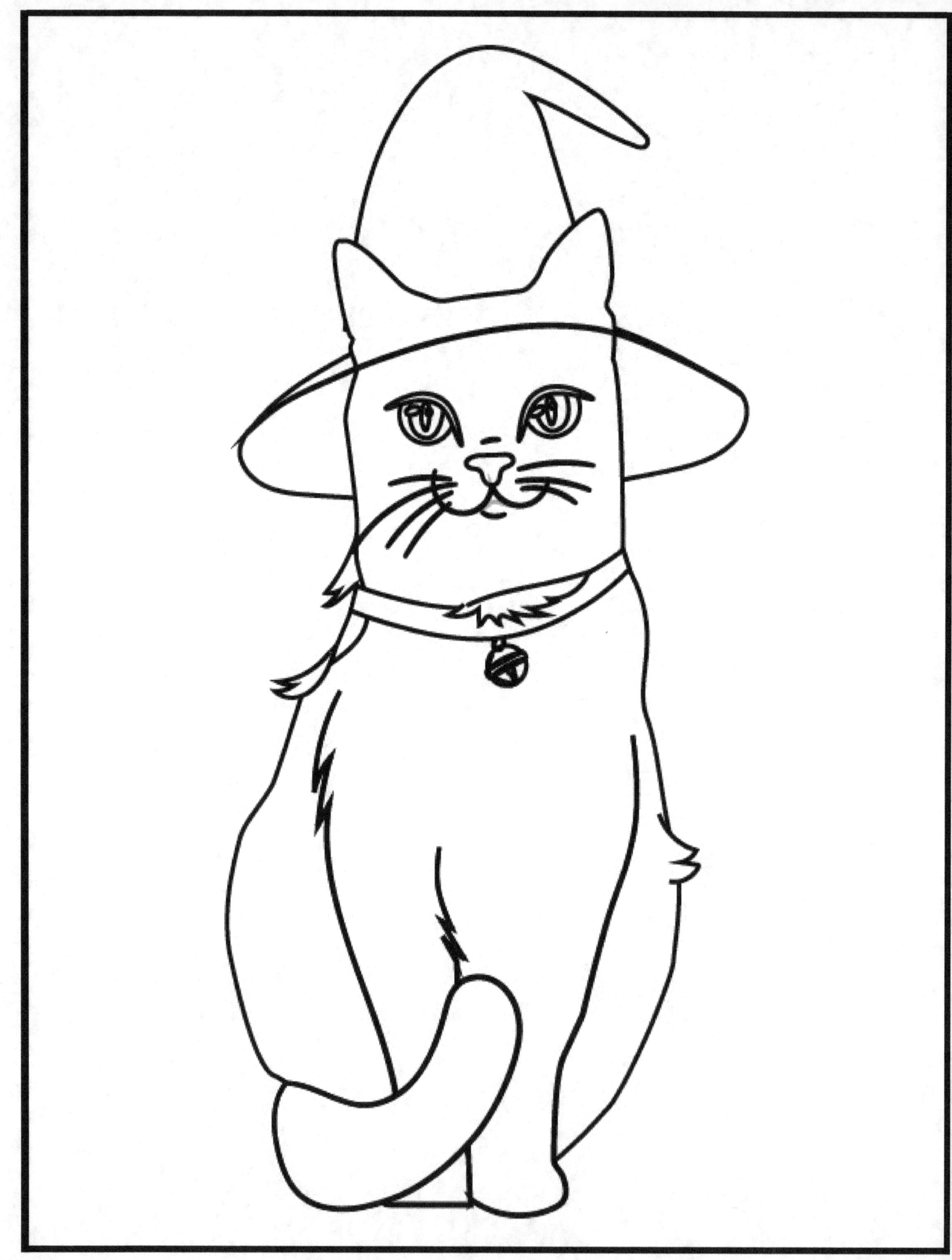

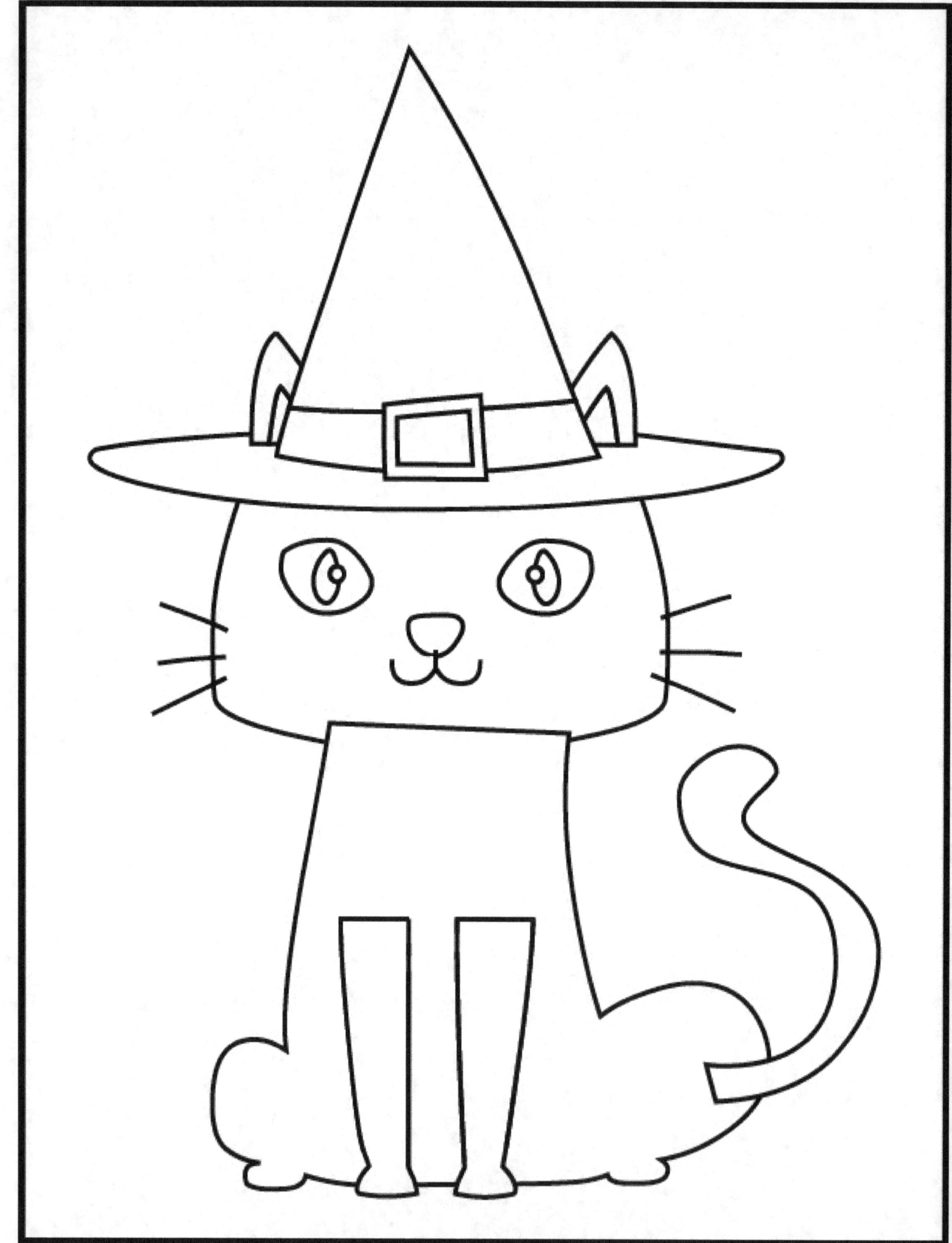

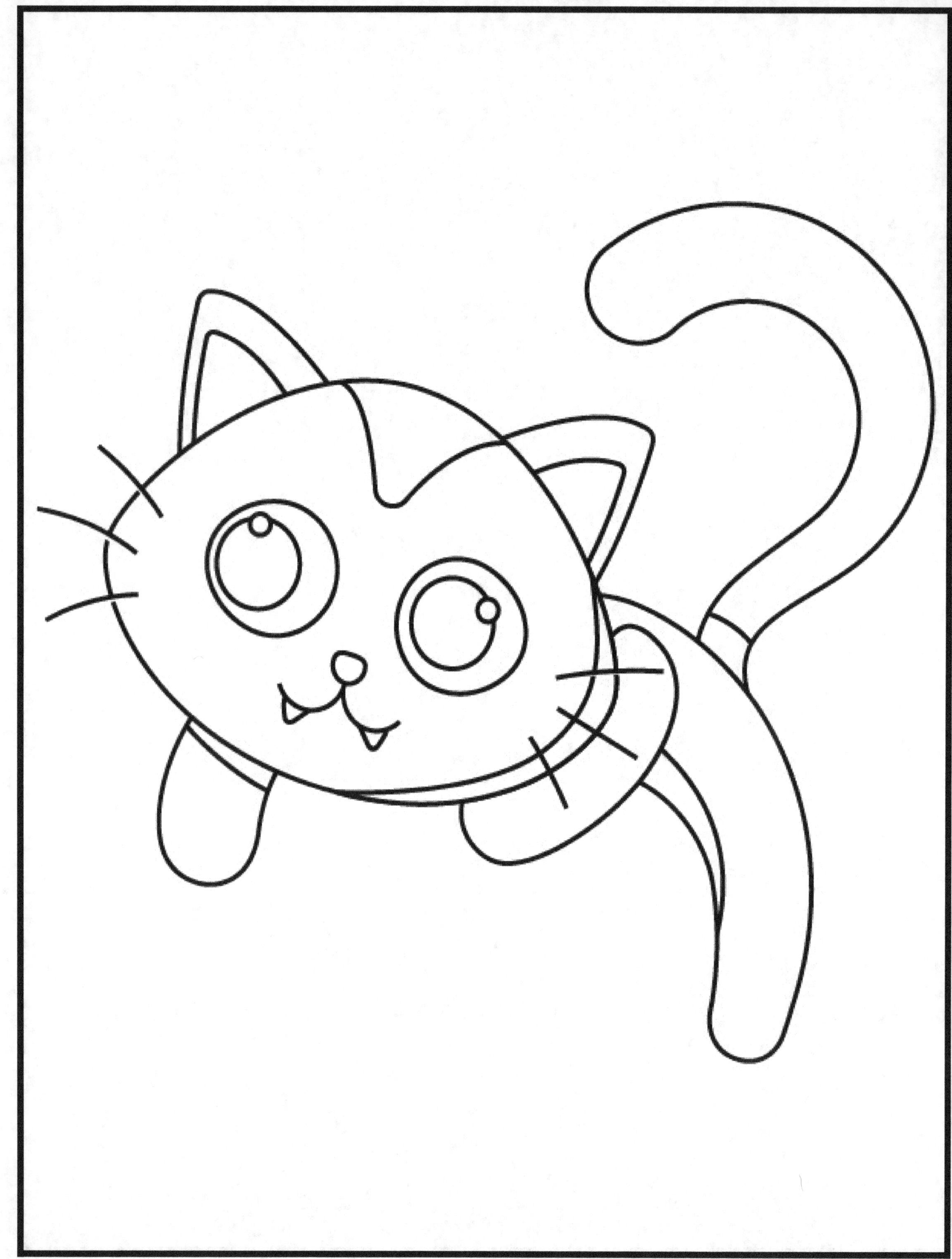

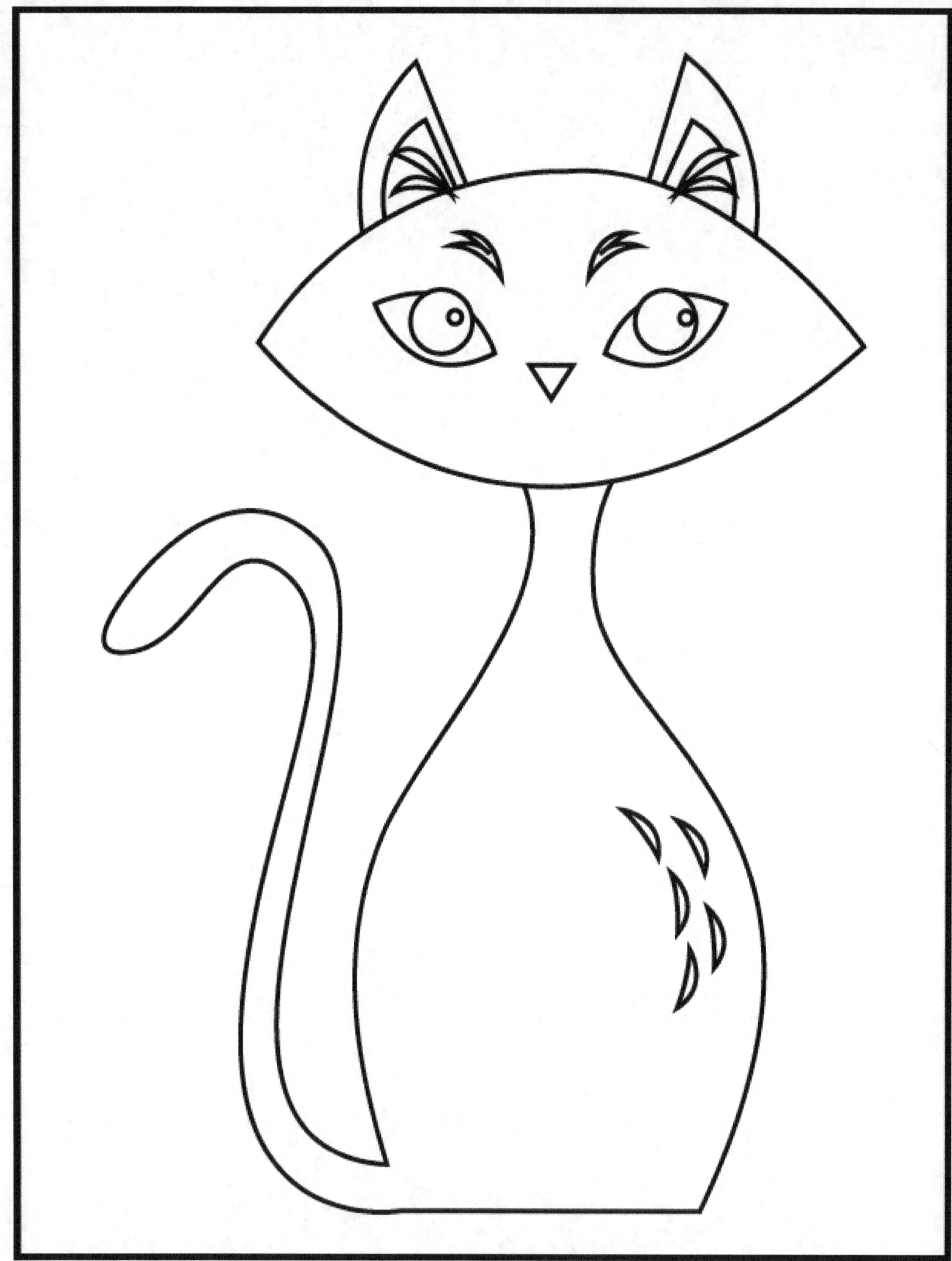